D0004778

SALLETS HUMBLES AND SHREWSBERY CAKES

A Collection of Elizabethan Recipes
Adapted for the Modern Kitchen

Sallets, Humbles & Shrewsbery Cakes

by Ruth Anne Beebe

With a Foreword by William Ingram

DAVID R. GODINE · PUBLISHER

David R. Godine, Publisher
306 DARTMOUTH STREET, BOSTON, MASSACHUSETTS 02116

ISBN 0–87923–195–5
LCC 76–14226

First Printing

PRINTED IN THE UNITED STATES OF AMERICA

Contents

Sauces

Sallets

Sweetes & Breads

Acknowledgments

THE Elizabethan and Jacobean books from which the recipes in this volume have been transcribed are in the collections of the Henry E. Huntington Library, San Marino, California, and the Bodleian Library, Oxford, England. I am grateful to the Director and Librarian of the Huntington Library for permission to reprint the recipes, and to the staff of the library, especially Mary Wright, for their constant kindness during my research there. I wish also to thank Ms. Kathleen Strickland, Professor William Ingram, Professor Arthur F. Kinney, and most of all, my husband to whom this book is dedicated.

R. B.

Foreword

FOOD AND SEX are generally recognized as the objects of our two strongest desires, but the Elizabethans, unlike modern Americans, seem to have had handbooks only for the former. Even Sir Hugh Plat's *Delights for Ladies*, despite its title, is intended primarily for the kitchen. I say "primarily," because the contents of such books as *Delights for Ladies* or *The Dyetary of Helth* or *The Huswifes Treasury* differ from the contents of a modern cookbook in ways that reflect the altered functions of both the kitchen and the cook. The Elizabethan books contained, like our own, recipes for the preparation of meats and vegetables; but they also were expected to describe—and the more ambitious of them did describe at length—ways of making ale and various mulled wines, recipes for the preparation of household medicines, procedures for the distillation of perfumes, and instructions on making candles and soap.

Under medicinal recipes, for example, one would be likely to find simple potions for upset stomach or for the headache, as well as directions for removing warts and spots. Occasionally an unexpected treasure can be found, such as a recipe for "A Sleeping Apple," to be made from "Opium, Mandrake, juice of Hemlock, and the Seeds of Henbane." The recipient of this compound is not, like Snow White, expected to eat it, but merely to hold it to his nose in an effort to induce slumber. One also finds, on occasion, certain "remedies against the Pox"—not smallpox or chicken pox, but the disease known as French pox, or syphilis. There is also a compound made of the powder of "Lithargy, Aloes, Frankincense, Verdigris, and Alum, beaten and mixed together with Oil of Mastic," to be rubbed on afflicted parts as a remedy "against Crab-lice."

Some remedies must have strained credulity even in their own day. As a cure for "the falling evil," or epilepsy, the reader of one book is advised to "take the blood of his little finger that is sick," to write certain Latin verses on a parchment with it, and to "hang them about his neck." The same book advises this remedy for "one that is bit with a dog": "write on a crust of cheese, Piga Cera Dera Effema, and give it to the sick to eat." Amusing nostrums of this sort are available in all cultures, including our own; we do not take them as the norm today, and we must be on our guard against taking them as an Elizabethan norm for the same reasons. They are old wives' tales, and the enlightened would have scoffed at them even while the booksellers were discovering that they had a market.

Even in the more conventionally culinary section of an

Elizabethan cookbook, one finds unfamiliar advice. The preservation of foods, taken by us for granted, was a major concern to the Elizabethan cook, and her cookbook would usually furnish guidance on "how to preserve flesh and fish," and caution her "how fruits must be shut up and kept close that the Air come not at them." A typical section on preservation might inform us that "figs may be preserved in Honey," the "Quinces may be preserved in Wine," "cucumbers in the Lees of wine," that "oranges may be kept in Cedar-dust," "apples may be kept in chaff," "mushrooms may be kept in millet-seed," and even that "flesh hanged on a Brazen-nail will keep long."

Such a brass nail as this last bit of advice calls for was, of course, no more common in an Elizabethan kitchen than it is in a modern kitchen, and the Elizabethan cook who was fortunate to have a chunk of meat large enough to require hanging would likely hang it from whatever was near to hand. The kitchen of the common man was, in Elizabethan times, no grand affair; at the lower end of the scale it might consist of no more than a place to build a fire, a large kettle, a tripod to hang it from, a ladle, a sharp knife, a mortar and pestle, and some plates. The cuisine emerging from such a kitchen was likely to be simple, and for the most part the compilers of cookbooks were not addressing themselves to this segment of the population. A more elaborate kitchen would be equipped with an assortment of strainers, graters, skimmers, copper pots and pans, chopping blocks, ovens, and roasting spits. These kitchens were in the minority, and money was invested in them precisely because their owners expected a more varied fare to emerge at mealtimes. The cook in such a kitchen was thus under a double obligation, to cook variously and to cook well, and the recipes in the more copious Elizabethan cookbooks were intended rather to serve his needs than the needs of the humbler cook.

It is a commonplace today that no cook is better than her raw ingredients. The Elizabethan cook, on the other hand, would have been viewed with suspicion if she could not rise above her ingredients, for they were neither as succulent nor as tempting as we might expect. The mythologizers who extol the simpler and more wholesome food of our forebears have perhaps blinded us to the fact that, on the whole, meats were tougher and less flavorful than today, and vegetables generally smaller and harder, as well as being available in fewer varieties. Thomas Coghan, in his *Haven of Helth*, reminds us that "it is said that a good Cook can make you good meat of a whetstone." Today we might substitute "of an old shoe," a sign of how our expectations have been raised.

One of the Elizabethan cook's remedies for the deficiencies of the ingredients lay in the imaginative use of spices, to heighten flavor or even to provide it. As many as a dozen herbs and spices might be called for in a single dish; most commonly used were salt, sugar, ginger, cinnamon, cloves, mace, parsley, onion, garlic, anise, fennel, nutmeg, mustard, saffron, cubebs, galingale, cumin, licorice, buckwheat, and pepper. Another remedy was the chopping or mincing of tough ingredients to make them more palatable. Most vegetables were treated in this fashion; and even meats, though they continued to be cooked and served in solid form, were also increasingly processed this way. More and more recipes came to call for the use of the mortar and pestle, and of the strainer. It may be useful to recall that the Elizabethan at table had only a knife, a spoon, and fingers with which to eat; the fork was, according to tradition, introduced by Thomas Coryat in the early seventeenth century on his return from a trip to Italy. Before the arrival and adoption of this new implement, the Elizabethan cook would be expected to tailor recipes to the utensils available for dining; hence the commonness of such dishes as "spoonbread" and "spoonmeat."

The recipes in this book provide a good cross-section of the skillful Elizabethan cook's repertory and also afford us a sense of the kinds of foods commonly served. The family fortunate enough to have a small garden was likely to devote a large portion of it to the growing of herbs, both savory and medicinal, and to cultivate only a limited range of vegetables, chiefly onions, garlic, leeks, radishes, lettuce, and cabbage. By the end of Elizabeth's reign, adventurous planters were experimenting with carrots, parsnips, turnips, and cucumbers, as well as yams brought back from North America. But these latter vegetables were slow to catch on, and the common potato, though probably known in England at this time, was flatly rejected as table fare. In general, the tastes of Shakespeare's contemporaries were probably not too different from those of Chaucer's Summoner, who "well loved garlic, onions and leeks." The diner of more sophisticated taste would seek ways to escape this syndrome, and his cook would in turn be driven to find more adventurous recipes.

In contrast to the limited range of vegetables, fruits were very common and quite popular. When Elizabeth first came to the throne, England was described by one writer as a "fruitful and plenteous region" where one might expect to find "wardens, quinces, peaches, medlars, chestnuts, and other delicious fruits serving for all seasons of the year, and so plenty of pears and apples that in the west parts of England and Sussex they make perry and cider, and in such abundance that they convey part over the sea, where by the Monsieurs of France it is coveted for their beverages and drinks." Apricots and cherries were also common and are mentioned by Shakespeare and other writers.

The commonest Elizabethan staples of all were meat and fish. One might offer a dinner with neither vegetables nor fruit, but a meal without meat or fish would have been unthinkable except to the impoverished. The meats found at table were as many and as varied as one's money could provide. Pork, beef, mutton, and venison were popular and were cooked many ways ranging from boiling and roasting to baking in a pie. Rabbit and wild fowl vied with the more domesticated chicken in popularity, and close behind came the tough but abundant pigeon. In a household of moderate means, when a few guests might be expected at table, the normal fare would consist of four or five dishes, mostly of meat, with the appropriate garnishing. Thus when Justice Shallow invites Falstaff to dinner, he orders "some pigeons, Davy; a couple of short-legged hens; a joint of mutton; and any pretty little tiny kickshaws, tell William Cook." The meal thus ordered is conventionally modest and would have been perfectly acceptable on certain days; on other days, unfortunately, it would have been illegal, odd though that seems. To understand this strange state of affairs, and its effect on the Elizabethan's diet, we must look to the government.

England was a maritime nation in the sixteenth century, and one way to insure a constant readiness both of ships and of seamen was to encourage the fishing industry. Robert Cecil, Elizabeth's Principal Secretary, urged that his government should "let the old course of fishing be maintained by the straitest observation of fish days for policy's sake; so the sea coasts could be strong with men and habitations and the fleet flourish more than ever." One way to expand an industry is to require the populace to consume its product; accordingly, more and more Fish Days were legislated "not for any religion or holiness supposed to be in the eating of fish rather than of flesh, but only for a civil policy," as Thomas Coghan observed at the time. All the forty days of Lent were fish days, as were also—in time—every Wednesday, Friday, and Saturday so that, by Coghan's reckoning (and with only a slight exaggeration), "one half of the year is ordained to eat fish in." This was a heavy regimen, and good public relations were necessary to keep it acceptable. The herring fishermen of Yarmouth engaged Thomas Nashe to write his *Lenten Stuffe* on their behalf. He says, only partly in jest,

> *A red herring is wholesome in a frosty morning; it is most precious fish-merchandise, because it can be carried through all Europe. Nowhere are they so well cured as at Yarmouth.*

The poorer sort make it three parts of their sustenance. It is every man's money, from the king to the peasant. The round, or cob, beaten to a powder, is a cure for the stone. A red herring drawn on the ground will lead hounds a false scent. A broiled herring is good for the rheumatism. The fishery is a great nursery for seamen, and brings more ships to Yarmouth than assembled at Troy to fetch back Helen.

It was, indeed, the English fishermen, fishing off the Grand Banks of Newfoundland, who were the first English settlers in North America. William Bradford, who came over on the Mayflower, describes in his journal how, at their landing in Massachusetts, "a certain Indian came boldly amongst them, and spoke to them in broken English, which they could well understand, but marvelled at it. At length they understood by discourse with him, that he was not of these parts, but belonged to the eastern parts, where some English ships came to fish, with whom he was acquainted, and could name sundry of them by their names, amongst whom he had got his language." The English had been fishing the area for years; the very name of Cape Cod, current as early as 1602, shows what feature of the area the English thought most noteworthy. Cod and haddock from these waters were salted down and delivered in large quantities to English markets an ocean away.

The English cook thus had available not only salted fish, dried fish, and pickled fish, but a fair assortment of fresh fish and shellfish as well. Fresh fish and shellfish were often prepared in the same way: boiled whole in salt water to which some wine had been added. Preserved fish might be made into soups, stews, or pies, herring pie and eel pie being the most common. Some fish were deemed unfit for direct consumption, having so little taste or substance that they were suitable only for boiling in a stockpot. Erasmus, who lived in England for a time shortly before Elizabeth's reign, wrote that "there is a kind of fish which is called in England *Stockfish*: it nourisheth no more than a stock." Thomas Coghan felt impelled to add: "Yet I have eaten of a pie made only with Stockfish which hath been very good, but the goodness was not so much in the fish as in the cookery," another allusion to the good cook's virtue of rising above unpromising ingredients.

The numerous fish days were, as might be imagined, a strain on the equanimity of all concerned, but the regulations were strictly enforced. Government agents patrolled the streets to catch offenders, and Thomas Middleton, a playwright of the period, has described such a scene, in which the two agents accost a man in the street:

FIRST AGENT: *By your leave Sir,*
We must see what you have under your Cloak there.

MAN: *Have? I have nothing.*

FIRST AGENT: *No! Do you tell us that? What makes this lump stick out then? We must see, Sir.*

MAN: *What will you see, Sir, a pair of Sheets, and two of my Wife's foul Smocks, going to the Washers?*

SECOND AGENT: *Oh, we love that sight well; you cannot please us better. (Looks under the man's cloak) What! Do you gull us? Call you these Shirts and Smocks?*

MAN: *Now a Pox choke you,*
You have cozened me and five of my wive's kindred
Of a good Dinner; we must make it up now
With Herrings and Milk-pottage.
FIRST AGENT: *'Tis all Veal!*

The agents, having confiscated the veal, then debate whether they might offer it to a local whore in return for her favors; they conclude they should not. The whore, in her turn, typifies for us yet another class of Elizabethan, the person who lives not in a home but only in lodgings: one room, perhaps two, but without a kitchen. For such people—and they were numerous, especially in London—public eating places, called Ordinaries, were set up, where one might find a variety of common dishes simply prepared and inexpensively priced. Chaucer's cook may well have been from such an establishment, for he had all the conventional virtues: "He could roast, and seethe, and broil, and fry,/Make mortreux, and well bake a pie." But for those who ate at Ordinaries, the fare was likely to be depressingly similar, even as it is today in similar establishments.

It is well for us to remind ourselves of these circumstances while remembering that a good household kitchen was an uncommon facility; for it must not be presumed that the recipes in this book furnish us any clue to the way the ordinary Elizabethan ate. The "average man" was no more a gourmet in Elizabethan England then he is in our own society, and consequently these recipes are as unreliable a guide to everyday Elizabethan fare as a good modern cookbook is to our own daily eating habits. What we may learn from these recipes—and it is knowledge eminently worth having—is how some of the people ate some of the time, whether on meat days or on fish days. Certainly this constitutes a kind of culinary elitism; but it is no more than the distinction between dining and eating, between cuisine and cooking. These recipes, and others like them, have survived because they were treasured; others have perished, many perhaps in their own day, and many perhaps for good reason.

WILLIAM INGRAM
Ann Arbor, Michigan

Introduction

Good Reader:
This cookbook is for your reading pleasure,
As well as your eating pleasure.
May you enjoy both, to full measure!

ELIZABETHAN COOKBOOKS bear little similarity to their modern counterparts. Many of the recipes are incomplete: instructions are often scanty and sometimes entirely omitted; quantities often as not are determined by "as your Cookes mouth shall serve him." They appear to be written as memory crutches to already knowledgeable cooks (or perhaps as a window through which the lower class could perceive the eating habits of the well-to-do). Recipes have no names. In the early books they frequently do not even have a defined beginning or end but run on rather like a narrative. Illustrations for guidance are almost completely lacking. It is clear that the Elizabethan cook did not share our present day obsession with nailing down quantities to the nearest quarter teaspoon. The rare exception to this rule is characterized by the fish recipe which calls for the outrageous ratio of one pound of butter to a pint of wine!

These books are endlessly fascinating to read; their language is full of color and surprise. A rabbit, for example, is apt to be called "she," and a duck "he." The cadence and ring of words were given far greater consideration than spelling or punctuation. One sometimes wishes that greater emphasis were placed on the accuracy of expression than the vividness of phrase. Orthography was, to put it mildly, flexible, and individual style came through very demonstrably in the concluding instructions in various recipes. One compiler directs that the dish be served "upon sops," another suggests "serve it upon sippets" and a third "serve it to the table hot."

The following collection presents a selection of recipes I have personally enjoyed cooking and eating. Quite a number of the recipes I found lend themselves poorly to updating; many are downright impractical for the modern kitchen. I have nevertheless included one or two that fall in this category. A perfect example is the recipe for frying "an egg round as a ball." It would be far easier to just fry up a batch of eggs, but the language in this recipe is irresistible, and the image of the end result seductive. Indeed, the method could well be applied to cooking eggs for a large group and keeping them warm before serving. One of my favorites explains simply how to serve fowl:

TO ROAST A CAPON, PHEASANT, OR PARTRIDGE

Roast a capon with his head off, his wings and legs on whole; and your Pheasant in like sort: but when you serve him in, stick one of his feathers upon his breast. And in like manner you must roast a Partridge, but stick up no feather.

All of the recipes in this book issue from four Tudor and early Stuart cookbooks: Thomas Dawson, *The Good Huswife's Iewell* (1596), *The Good Huswife's Handmaide for the Kitchin* (1594), Gervase Markam, *The English Huswife*, Book II of *Countrey Contentments* (1615), and John Murrell, *Delightful daily exercise for ladies and gentlewomen* (1621). In each case, the original version of the recipe appears first with the spelling unchanged, exactly as it was printed. There follows an adapted version, often involving slight but unavoidable compromises to modern tastes. The original recipes, however, are so eminently vague that there are any number of possible interpretations, and I would like to think that by unearthing these recipes I have inspired some readers to experiment on their own. The renditions given here *do* work, though, and should serve as guidelines for the less adventurous cook.

In each of the original cookbooks a great deal of space was devoted to recipes for meat, fish, and fowl, not surprising since the Elizabethans ate meat at virtually every meal (and were consequently often afflicted with the gout). Many of the meat recipes call for hours of boiling. This no doubt results from the poor quality of Elizabethan meat, and the unsavory fact that it was often spoiled by the time it reached the pot. Dozens of herbs and spices were added, partly to disguise the rancid flavor, but also because spices were new, exotic, and exciting. Today's ingredients are a good deal fresher than those the Elizabethans had to work with, and cooking times in the adaptations have been reduced accordingly. Vegetable recipes are relatively rare, but because of modern food preferences I have included most that I found. Following the recipes is a page of sample menus for those interested in recreating an entire Elizabethan meal.

The ingredients used in these recipes are readily available most everywhere. Of course, fresh meats, vegetables, and herbs are preferable, but frozen or dried foods will do in a pinch. Rose and violet petals may be purchased in organic food shops; rosewater is available in most pharmacies; ale can be bought in any liquor store. Venison is not sold in many states, and if this is the case where you live, veal makes an adequate alternative. Some of the whole spices specified may be difficult to find, but since most recipes call for them to be crushed, ground spices can be substituted.

Many of the dessert recipes are intended as much for decoration as for sustenance. One "recipe" I found consists of a sampling of all the colorful garden flowers gaily assembled into a showy centerpiece. The recipe included in this book for "snowe" is intended primarily for display, but also constitutes a tasty dessert.

The English avidly and voluminously consumed bread, wine, and beer. However, recipes for these staples are generally missing in Tudor cookbooks. The beverages were readily available in shops and taverns; larger households often baked bread and brewed beer a year's supply at a time. I have included here a recipe for "manchet", a very *substantial* bread, and considered by the Elizabethans one of their finest. The quantities in this recipe have been greatly reduced to yield but one loaf. The other "breads" presented here more closely resemble cookies or tea cakes; they make a fine breakfast or snack. They are heavier and crunchier than their modern counterparts, perhaps because they were often kept for long periods or were packed for picnics or long journeys. For those wishing to brew their own beer, there is this recipe:

FOR THE BREWING OF ORDINARY BEER,
Your malt being well ground and put in your Mash-fat, and your liquor in your lead ready to boil, you shall then by little and little with scoops or pails put the boiling liquor to the malt, and then stir it even to the bottom exceedingly well together (which is called the mashing of the malt), then the liquor swimming in the top cover all over with more malt, and so let it stand an hour and more in the mash-fat, during which space you may if you please heat more liquor in your lead for your second or small drink. This done, pluck up your mashing stoum, and let the first liquor run gently from the malt, either in a clean trough or other vessels prepared for the purpose, and then stopping the mash-fat again, put the second liquor to the malt and stir it well together; then your lead being emptied, put your first liquor or wort therein and then to every quarter of malt, put a pound and a half of the best hops you can get, and boil them an hour together until taking up a dishful thereof, you can see the hops shrink into the bot-

tom of the dish. This done, put the wort through a strait sieve which may drain the hops from it into your cooler, which standing over the Gill-fat you shall in the bottom thereof set a great bowl with your barm and some of the first wort (before the hops come into it mixed together) that it may rise therein, and then let your wort drop or run gently into the dish with the barm which stands in the Guil-fat, and this you shall do the first day of your brewing, letting your collar drop all the night following, and some part of the next morning, and as it droppeth, if you find that a black scum or lumps riseth upon the barm, you shall with your hand take it off and cast it away. Then, nothing being left in the cooler, and the beer well risen, with your hand stir it about and so let it stand an hour after, and then beating it and the barm exceeding well together, tun (bottle) it up in the Hogshead, being clean washed and scalded, and so let it purge. And herein you shall observe not to tun your vessels too full for fear thereby it purge too much of the barm away. When it hath purged a day and a night, you shall close up the bungholes with clay, and only for a day or two after, keep a vent-hole in it; and after close it up as close as may be. Nor for your second or small drink which are left upon the grains, you shall suffer it there to stay, but an hour or a little better, and then drain it off also, which done, put it into the lead with the former hops and boil the other also. Then clear it from the hops and cover it very close till your first beer be tunned, and then as before put it also to barm and so tun it up also in smaller vessels. And of this second beer you shall not draw above one Hogshead to three of the better. Now there be diverse other ways and observations for the brewing of ordi-

nary Beer, but none so good, so easy, so ready and quickly performed as this before shown. Neither will any beer last longer or ripen sooner, for it may be drunk at a fortnight age and will last as long and lively.

Elizabethan cookbooks also provided a wellspring of remedies. Although modern tradition says they have no place in a cookbook, I could not resist including the following three:

FOR THE PIN AND WEB IN THE EYE
Take the juice of Parsley and half as much honey, and with a feather drop it in the eye and after it you must put in some powder of white sugar candy. You must dress it thus very often.

TO TAKE AWAY THE POCK-HOLES OR ANY SPOT IN THE FACE
Take white rosewater, and wet a fine cloth therein, and set it all night to freeze, and then lay it upon your face till it be dry. Also take three poppies, the reddest you can get, and quarter them, taking out the garbage. Then still them in a quart of new milk of a red cow, & with the water thereof wash your face.

FOR THE GOUT THAT IS NEWLY COME
Take Rhubarb, and grate it, and mingle it with conserve of red roses, and eat thereof every morning, fasting a pretty quantity.

Elizabethan banquets were no small affairs. A household of twenty or more was often fed, not to mention relatives and guests, servants and children. The meal consisted of a vast variety of dishes—with as many as twenty different kinds of meat all placed on the table at once. Each person had a trencher, or square wooden plate hollowed out like a bowl, a large spoon, and a knife. With these, he helped himself to whatever he wanted, carving with his knife, tearing with his hands and eating, or rather gorging, with spoon and fingers. The most important guest was always served first. If the food was not entirely consumed in the main household and by the guests, it was served to the relatives, then the household staff and, finally, to the poor who waited outside the house for left-overs and scraps.

Salt was frequently added at the last minute and was "strewed on" as the food went to the table. In Elizabeth's time a salt shaker was always placed on the table, and the person seated next to it was considered the least important of the guests. His task was to pass it constantly!

I hope that both the seasoned and the occasional cook will try these recipes with as much relish as I. We should all welcome the opportunity to partake of a good, groaning board of Tudor food.

RUTH BEEBE
Lancaster, California

SALLETS
HUMBLES
AND
SHREWSBERY
CAKES

Flesh

To bake Venison

Perboyle your Venison, then season it with Pepper and salt, somewhat grose beaten, and a little Ginger, and good store of sweete Butter. Add when the Venison is tender baked: put to it halfe a dozen spoonfuls of Claret wine and shake it well together.

✣ ✣ ✣

4 half-pound venison steaks
 (or veal steaks)
6 tablespoons butter
1 teaspoon salt
1 teaspoon freshly ground pepper
1 teaspoon ginger
½ cup dry red wine

Place the venison in one layer in an ovenproof dish. Dot the steaks with the butter and sprinkle with salt, pepper and ginger. Bake in a preheated 350° oven for 40 minutes. Add the wine and bake for an additional 10 minutes or until the meat is done through.

Serves 4

To boyle Mutton en Steau

Take a Legge or a Loine of Mutton, cut either of them in 3 or 4 pieces, set them on in a gallon of faire water, and when it boyleth skumme it, then put in three or foure blades of mace, grose Pepper, whole Cloves, a little Salt, sixe whole Onions, let it boyle close covered an houre, then take a handfull of Parsley, a handfull of Spinage, a handfull of Sorrell, halfe a handfull of Savory and Thime stript, three or foure Onions slict, and shred them very small, then put them into your boyling mutton with halfe an ounce of grated bread, and let it boile something softly, untill it comes from a gallon to a pottle, then dish it very neatly up upon sippets and strew Salt upon it and serve it to the table hot.

✣ ✣ ✣

3 pounds lamb loin, cut in 2–3-inch strips
1 tablespoon each whole peppercorns, whole cloves
1 teaspoon mace
1 cup dry red wine
1 cup each chopped parsley, fresh spinach and celery
4 medium onions, cut in quarters
1 teaspoon each savory and thyme
2 teaspoons salt
1 cup fresh bread crumbs

Place the lamb in a large pot and cover with water. Boil for 20 minutes, then skim off the fat. Add the mace. Put the pepper and cloves in a tea ball and add to the lamb. Cover and simmer for an hour. Add the wine, parsley, spinach, celery, onions, savory, thyme and salt. Simmer, uncovered, until the onions are tender and the liquid is reduced (about 30 minutes). Add bread crumbs and serve in bowls.

Serves 6

To roste a Hare

First wash it in faire water, then perboyle it and lay in cold water againe, then larde it, and roste it on a broch. Then to make sauce for it, take red Vinigar, Salt, Pepper, Ginger, Cloves, Mace, and put them together. Then minse Apples, and Onions, and frie them in a pan: then put your sawce to them with a litle Sugar, and let them boyle well together, then baste it upon your Hare, and so serve it foorth.

✤ ✤ ✤

3 pounds rabbit, whole or cut into serving pieces
butter
½ cup wine vinegar
1 teaspoon salt
½ teaspoon freshly ground pepper
2 apples, cored and cut into eighths
1 small onion, finely chopped
1 tablespoon sugar
¼ teaspoon each ginger, cloves and mace

Place the rabbit in a large pot, cover with water and parboil for 30 minutes. Drain and rinse in cold water. Rub the rabbit with butter and place in a roasting pan. Bake in a 400° oven for 20 minutes. Turn down the heat to 350° and roast for an additional 40 minutes. Prepare the sauce by simmering the wine vinegar, salt, pepper, apples, onion, sugar and spices. Baste the meat often during roasting. When the rabbit is done pour over the remaining sauce and serve.

Serves 4

To make stewed Steakes

Take a peece of Mutton, and cutte it in peeces, and washe it very cleane, and put it into a faire potte with Ale, or with halfe Wine, then make it boyle, and skumme it cleyne, and put into your pot a faggot of Rosemary and Time, then take some Parsely picked fine, and some onyons cut round, and let them all boyle together, then take prunes, & raisons, dates, and currans and let it boyle altogether, and season it with Sinamon and Ginger, Nutmeggs, two or three Cloves, and Salt, and so serve it on soppes, and garnish it with fruite.

✣ ✣ ✣

2 pounds lamb stew meat cut into cubes
1 pint beer or ale
2 teaspoons rosemary
1 tablespoon thyme
½ cup parsley, chopped
2 medium onions, sliced into rings
2 oranges and 2 lemons, peeled and quartered
8 prunes and 8 dates, chopped
½ cup raisins
¼ cup currants
¼ teaspoon each cinnamon, ginger, cloves and nutmeg
orange and lemon slices for garnish

Place the lamb in a large pot, cover with the beer and simmer for about a half hour. Skim off any excess fat that rises to the surface. Add the rosemary, thyme, parsley and onions and simmer for 15 minutes. Then add the fruit and spices and simmer an additional 10–15 minutes. Serve over fried bread (page 66) and garnish with the orange and lemon slices.

Serves 6

To stew Fillets of Beefe

Take a rawe fillet of beefe and cut it in thin slices halfe as broad as your hand and fry them till they bee halfe fried in a frying panne with sweete butter uppon each side with a soaft fire, then powre them into a dish or pipkin putting in a pint of claret-wine, a faggot of sweete herbes, and two or three blades of whole mace, a little salt the meate of a Lemon cut in slices, then stewe these all together very softly for the space of two or three houres till it be halfe boyled away, then dish it upon sippets and throwe salt upon it, and serve it to the table hot.

✣ ✣ ✣

2 pounds sirloin filets, cut into strips
4 tablespoons butter
1 cup dry sherry
1 teaspoon rosemary
1 tablespoon each thyme and sage
1 teaspoon mace
1 teaspoon salt
freshly ground pepper
juice of ½ lemon
½ cup water

Melt the butter in a heavy skillet and brown the meat well on all sides. Add the remaining ingredients. Simmer, covered, for one hour or until the meat is tender. Stir occasionally and add more liquid if necessary. Serve over fried bread. Top each serving with a wedge of lemon.

Serves 6

To roste Olives of Veale

You shall take a legge of veale and cut the flesh from the bones, and cut it out into thin long slices; then take sweete hearbes and the white parts of scallions, and chop them well together with the yolkes of egges, then rowle it up within the slices of veale, and so spit them and roast them; then boile verjuice, butter, sugar, cynamon, currants and sweet hearbes together, and being seasoned with a little salt, serve the Olives up upon that sauce with salt cast over them.

✣ ✣ ✣

1½–2 pounds veal, sliced into 4 very thin cutlets
2 egg yolks, slightly beaten
1½ teaspoons each marjoram, thyme, basil and parsley
1 tablespoon scallions or chives, chopped
1 teaspoon salt

Sauce:
½ cup (1 stick) butter
1 teaspoon cinnamon
2 tablespoons currants
1½ teaspoons each parsley and fresh basil, finely chopped
2 tablespoons lemon juice or white wine
¼ teaspoon salt

Place the veal on a flat ovenproof pan with a rim and brush the egg yolks over the surface of the meat. Mix herbs and sprinkle evenly on each cutlet. Roll the cutlets and fasten them with skewers or toothpicks. Prepare the sauce by melting the butter, adding the remaining ingredients and simmering just until the currants soften. Bake the veal at 350° for 20 minutes, basting often with the sauce. Pour any remaining sauce over the meat and serve immediately. *Serves 4*

To stue Beefe

Take Beefe and smyte it in peeces, and wash it in faire water, and draine that water and put it in the potte with the Beefe, and boyle them together. Then take Pepper, Cloves, Mace, Onions, Parsley and Sage, cast it thereto and let it boyle together: Then make licquor with bread and thicke it: and so let it seethe a good while after that the thicking is in. Then put in Saffron, Salt and vinegar, and so serve it forth.

✣ ✣ ✣

1 tablespoon each butter and oil
2 pounds beef stew meat, cubed
beef stock
1 medium onion, chopped
1 tablespoon parsley, chopped
¼ teaspoon each sage and mace
½ teaspoon cloves
1 teaspoon salt
½ teaspoon freshly ground pepper
2 slices stale bread, cubed
1 tablespoon wine vinegar
pinch of saffron

In a dutch oven heat the oil and butter. Brown the meat well on all sides, then add beef stock to cover. Add the onion, parsley, sage, mace, cloves, salt and pepper and simmer, covered, for 45 minutes to one hour. Just before serving stir in the bread, vinegar and saffron. Serve in bowls.

Serves 4

To fry Bakon

Cut your bakon as thinne as a card and parboyle it, then fry it in a panne without any liquor upon a very coole fire, then fry them good and browne on the other side, then take them up and put them in a warme dish and set them by the fire and it will be very crispe and never rise in the stomake, then dish up your egs in a warme dish and lay the bakon all over them cover them with a dish, and serve them to the table hot.

✣ ✣ ✣

4 thin slices of bacon per person
poached eggs

Place the bacon in a pot of water and boil for 5 minutes to cook off some of the fat and prevent sticking during frying. Remove to a frying pan. Cook over low heat for two or three minutes on each side. Remove from the heat, place on a fire-resistent serving dish and keep warm in a 250° oven while poaching the eggs. Lay the bacon over the eggs and serve.

Serves 4

To boile Mutton and Chickens

Take your mutton and Chickens and sette uppon the fire with faire water and when it is well skummed, take two handfull of Cabadge, Lettice, a handfull of currants a good peece of butter, the juice of two or three Lemmons, a good deale of grosse Pepper and a good peece of Suger, and let them seeth all well together, then take three or foure yolkes of egges togeather harde rosted, and straine them with parte of your broth, let them seeth a quantitye of an houre. Serve your broth with meate uppon Sippets.

✤ ✤ ✤

1½ pounds chicken, boned and cut into serving pieces
1 pound lamb stew meat, cubed
2 cups chicken broth
½ head cabbage, cut into wedges
½ head Boston lettuce, chopped
4 hard boiled egg yolks, mashed
½ cup currants
2 tablespoons butter
1 teaspoon salt
¼ teaspoon ginger
¼ teaspoon nutmeg
½ teaspoon freshly ground pepper
juice of two lemons
¼ cup sugar

In a dutch oven brown the chicken and lamb well on all sides. Add the chicken broth, cover and simmer for 30 minutes. Skim off any excess fat that rises to the surface. Take ½ cup of the broth and add to it the egg yolks, stirring until the mixture is smooth. Return the mixture to the meat and add the remaining ingredients. Simmer 30 minutes more or until the meat is very tender. Serve in bowls over fried bread (page 66) with plenty of broth.

Serves 6

Fish

To seeth fresh Salmon

Take a little water, and as much Beere and Salt, and put thereto Parsley, Time, and Rosemarie, and let all these boyle together: then put in your Salmon, and make your broth sharpe with some Vinigar.

* * *

- 2 pounds salmon steaks or fileted salmon
- 2 tablespoons butter
- 2 cups beer
- 1 teaspoon salt
- freshly ground pepper
- ½ cup parsley, chopped
- 1 tablespoon thyme
- ½ teaspoon rosemary
- ¼ cup white vinegar

Place the salmon in a heavy skillet, add the butter and cover with the beer. Simmer for several minutes, then add the salt, pepper to taste, parsley, thyme and rosemary. Simmer an additional 15 minutes or until the fish is tender and flakes easily. Add the vinegar and heat briefly. Arrange the fish on a serving dish and cover with the broth. This recipe also works very well if cooked in a crock pot.

Serves 4

To stew Flounders

Take two faire Flounders, cut off the heads and finnes, crosse them overthwart with a sharp knife two or three cuts then put them in a pewter dish the wite side downeward, put in halfe a pint of sweete butter, halfe a pint of vinegar, a handfull of shred parsley, three or foure blades of Mace, a faggot of sweete herbes, three or foure whole Onions, strow on a little salt, and let them stewe halfe an houre, then turne them and let them stew halfe an houre more, then dish it upon sippets and strewe salt upon it, and then serve it to the table hott.

✣ ✣ ✣

- 2 pounds whole flounder, heads and tails removed
- ½ cup (1 stick) butter, melted
- ⅓ cup cider vinegar
- 4 medium onions, coarsely chopped
- ½ cup fresh parsley, chopped
- 2 teaspoons mace
- ¼ teaspoon each allspice, basil and thyme
- 2 tablespoons sugar

Place the fish in a heavy skillet. Pour over it the melted butter and the vinegar. Add the onions, parsley, herbs and spices and simmer for 20 minutes. Turn the fish, add the sugar, and cook an additional 20 minutes or until the fish flakes easily and the onion is tender. Serve over fried bread (page 66).

Serves 4

To boile a Breame

Take White wine and put it into a pot, and let it seeth, then take your breame and cut him in the midst, and put him in, then take an Onion and chop it small, then take nutmegs beaten, cinamon and ginger, whole mace, and a pound of butter, and let it boile altogether, and so season it with salt, serve it uppon soppes, and garnish it with fruite.

✣ ✣ ✣

2 pounds filet of turbot
2 cups sweet white wine
1 medium onion, finely chopped
1 teaspoon each ground nutmeg, cinnamon, ginger and mace
½ teaspoon salt
freshly ground pepper
½ cup (1 stick) butter
fresh fruit

Turbot is the authentic fish for this recipe; however, if none is available, any other white fish such as sole will taste excellent. Place the fish in a heavy skillet and cover with the wine. Bring to a low boil and add the onion, spices, salt, pepper to taste and butter. Simmer, uncovered, for about 20 minutes or until the onion is tender and the fish flakes easily. Serve over fried bread (page 66) and with plenty of fresh fruit.

Serves 4

To bake a Trout

Wash it a litle, and take two or three Eles, a few Cloves, Mace, ginger, and Salt, and season the Trowt and the Ele together, and put them in the coffin together, and a few corrans about it, and a quantitie of Butter, and let them bake an houre and a halfe.

⁜ ⁜ ⁜

2 10-ounce trout, cleaned
2 10-ounce eels, cleaned
¼ teaspoon ground cloves
⅛ teaspoon each mace and ginger
½ teaspoon salt
freshly ground pepper
¼ cup fish stock
3 tablespoons butter
¼ cup currants
2 tablespoons dry sherry
pastry for a two-crust 9-inch pie

Place the trout and eels in a saucepan, cover with water and simmer for 15 minutes. Remove the fish from the liquid, skin and bone them and dice the meat. Blend in the spices, salt, stock, currants and sherry and arrange in the unbaked pie shell. Dot with butter and cover with second crust. Seal the edges and prick the top to allow steam to escape. Bake in a preheated 350° oven for 40 minutes or until the crust is golden brown. Eel makes the pie rich, but if it is not available, a moist fish such as mackerel will make a tasty substitute.

Serves 4

Fowle

To boile a Capon with Orenges and Lemmons

Take Orenges or Lemmons pilled, and cutte them the long way, and if you can keepe your cloves whole and put them into your best broth of Mutton or Capon with prunes and currants and three or fowre dates, and when these have beene well sodden put whole pepper, great mace, a good peece of suger, and some rose water, and either white or claret Wine, and let all these seeth together a while, & so serve it upon soppes with your capon.

✣ ✣ ✣

- 2½ pounds chicken, cut into serving pieces
- 1 tablespoon each oil and butter
- 1½ cups chicken stock
- 1 teaspoon rosewater
- 1 cup sweet white wine
- 2 oranges and 2 lemons, peeled and cut into eighths
- 8 prunes, chopped coarsely
- 8 dates, chopped coarsely
- ½ cup currants
- ¼ teaspoon salt
- ½ teaspoon whole peppercorns
- ½ tablespoon mace
- ½ teaspoon whole cloves

In a large skillet or dutch oven heat the oil and butter. Season the chicken pieces with salt and brown well on all sides. Add the chicken stock, rosewater and wine and simmer for 20 minutes. Add the fruit, salt, pepper, mace and cloves and continue to simmer another 15 minutes or until the chicken is tender. Serve over fried bread (page 66) with plenty of broth.

Serves 4

To boyle Chickens with Sparagus

Boyle your Chickens in faire water, with a little whole mace, put into their bellies a little parsley, and a little sweete butter, dish them upon sippets and powre a little of the same broath upon it, and take a hand-full of sparagus being boyled, and put them into a Ladle full of thicke butter, and stir it together in a dish, and powre it upon your Chickens or pullets, strew on salt, and serve it to the Table hot.

✣ ✣ ✣

1 tablespoon each oil and butter
2 pounds chicken, cut into serving pieces
salt and freshly ground pepper
½ cup chicken stock
½ cup dry white wine
½ cup parsley, chopped
½ teaspoon each mace, cinnamon
¼ teaspoon ginger
1 pound fresh asparagus

In a deep skillet heat the oil and butter. Season the chicken pieces with salt and pepper to taste and brown them well on all sides. Add the chicken stock, wine, parsley, mace, cinnamon and ginger and simmer, covered, for about 40 minutes or until the chicken is tender. Fifteen minutes before the chicken is done, place the asparagus in boiling water, cover, and simmer until tender. Drain the asparagus and arrange on a serving platter around the chicken pieces. Pour the sauce over chicken and asparagus and serve.

Serves 4

To frie Chickins

Take your chickins and let them boyle in verye good sweete broath a prittye while, and take the chickens out, and quarter them out in peeces, and then put them into a Frying pan with sweete butter, and let them stewe in the pan, but you must not let them be browne with frying, and then put out the butter out of the pan, and then take a little sweete broath, and as much Vergious, and the yolkes of two Egges, and beate them together, and put in a little Nutmegges, synamon and Ginger, and Pepper into the sauce, and then put them all into the pan to the chickens, and stirre them together in the pan, and put them into a dish, and serve them up.

✣ ✣ ✣

3 tablespoons butter
2–3 pounds chicken, cut into serving pieces
2 cups chicken stock
2 egg yolks
1 teaspoon each nutmeg and cinnamon
¼ teaspoon each ginger and freshly ground pepper
1 teaspoon salt
½ cup unsweetened apple juice

Melt the butter in a heavy skillet or dutch oven. Brown the chicken pieces well on all sides. Add the chicken stock and heat. Take ¼ cup of the stock and add it to the egg yolks, stir well and return this mixture to the chicken. Add the remaining ingredients, cover, and simmer for 40 minutes or until the chicken is tender.

Serves 4

To boyle a Mallard with Carets and Onyons

Take a Mallard being halfe roasted, and cut her up as you doe to eate them, put her into a pipkin with the brest downeward put to her two or three sliced Onyons, and Carrets, sliced square the bignesse of a Butchers prick, an inch long, a little grose pepper, a little salt, a little whole mace, a piece of sweete butter, a little parsley, a little savory and time, a pint of strong broath, a quarter of a pint of white wine: let these boyle halfe a way very softly, then dish up your Ducke upon sippets, and powre your broath on the toppe, and serve it hot to the Table.

✤ ✤ ✤

- 1 3–4-pound duck, cut into serving pieces
- 2 cups chicken stock
- 2 teaspoons salt
- 1 teaspoon whole peppercorns
- 1 teaspoon mace
- 1 cup parsley, chopped
- 2 tablespoons fresh savory
- 2 teaspoons thyme
- 3 medium onions, sliced thinly
- 5 carrots, sliced
- ¾ cup dry white wine

In a dutch oven brown the duck pieces well on all sides until the skin is very crisp. Pierce the skin with a skewer to allow the fat to drain. Pour off the fat and add the chicken stock, salt, peppercorns, mace, parsley, herbs, onions and carrots to the duck. Simmer, covered, for one hour. Add the wine and simmer for an additional 30 minutes or until the meat is very tender. Serve in large bowls over fried bread (page 66).

Serves 4

To boile a Capon in white Broth with Almondes

Take your Capon with marie bones and set them on the fire, and when they be cleane skummed take the fattest of the broth, and put it in a little pot with a good deale of marie, prunes, raisons, dates, whole maces, & a pinte of white wine, then blanch your almondes and strain them, with them thicken your potte & let it seeth a good while and when it is enough serve it uppon soppes with your capon.

✣ ✣ ✣

1 tablespoon each oil and butter
2½ pounds chicken, cut in serving pieces
2½ cups chicken stock
¼ cup raisins
8 prunes, chopped
8 dates, chopped
2 teaspoons mace
½ cup white wine
½ cup blanched and slivered almonds
salt and freshly ground pepper to taste

Heat the oil and butter in a heavy skillet or dutch oven. Season the chicken with salt and pepper and brown it well on all sides. Add the stock, cover and simmer for 30 minutes. Add the fruit, mace and wine and simmer for 20 minutes. Stir in the almonds and serve in bowls over fried bread (page 66).

Serves 4

To boyle a Capon or Chicken with Colle-flowres

Out of the budds of your flowres, boile them in milke with a little Mace, till they be very tender: then take the yolkes of two eggs straine them with a quarter of a pint of Sacke, then take as much thicke butter being drawne, with a little vinegar and a sliced Lemmon, and brue them together, then take the flowers out of the Milke, and put them into the Butter and Sacke, then dish up your Capon, being tender boyld, upon sippets, strowing a little salt upon it, and so poure on the sawce upon it, and so serve it to the Table hotte.

✤ ✤ ✤

1 tablespoon each butter and oil
salt
freshly ground pepper
2–3 pounds chicken, cut into serving pieces
2 cups chicken stock
1 head cauliflower
2 cups milk
2 tablespoons mace
½ cup (1 stick) butter
2 egg yolks
¼ cup dry sherry
2 teaspoons cider vinegar
juice of 1 lemon

In a heavy skillet heat the butter and oil. Season the chicken with salt and pepper to taste and brown it well on all sides. Add the chicken stock, cover, and simmer until tender (about 40 minutes). Twenty minutes before the chicken is done remove the outer leaves from the cauliflower, divide it into buds and place it in a large saucepan. Cover with the milk, add the mace and simmer until tender. Melt the butter in a small saucepan and add the egg yolks, sherry, vinegar and lemon juice. Stir until well blended. Drain the cauliflower, reserving the milk for another use. Add the butter mixture to the cauliflower, heat briefly and toss until all the buds are well coated. Arrange the chicken on a serving plattter and cover with the cauliflower. Serve over fried bread (page 66.)

Serves 4

Egges

To make Egs upon Sops

Take Egs and potche them as soft as ye can, then take a fine manchet, and make soppes thereof, and pùt your sops in a dish, and put vergious thereto and Sugar and a litle Butter: then set it to the fire, and let it boyle: then take your egs and lay them upon your Sops, and cast a litle chopt Parslie uppon them; and so serve them in.

✣ ✣ ✣

4 thick slices of white bread or manchet (page 63)
4 tablespoons butter
2 tablespoons unsweetened apple juice
1 tablespoon sugar
4 eggs
1 tablespoon vinegar
2 tablespoons parsley, chopped

In a heavy skillet melt the butter and add the fruit juice. Fry the bread slices until each side is nicely browned. Sprinkle with sugar. Poach the eggs in rapidly boiling water to which you have added the vinegar. Carefully place one egg on each slice of bread, sprinkle with parsley and serve hot.

Serves 4

To butter Egges of the best Fashion

Boyle your Egges very hard, and then blanch them in cold water, then slice them as thinne as wafers then you may take sweete butter drawne thicke with faire water, then season your Egges with a little grose Pepper, and salt, and then put them into your thicke butter, and so let them upon a Chafindish of char-coales, now and then tossing and turning them upside downe, then you may dish them up in a very faire dish, and prick fryed toastes about them: then strew on them a little grose pepper and salt, and so you may serve them to the Table hot.

✣ ✣ ✣

2 hardboiled eggs per person
1 tablespoon butter per two eggs
salt and freshly ground pepper
1 slice fried bread (page 66) per person

Slice the eggs very thinly. In a skillet melt the butter, add the egg slices and season with salt and pepper to taste. Stir gently with a spatula until the eggs are well coated with butter and heated through. Serve over fried bread.

To make a Quelquechose

To make a Quelquechose which is a mixture of many things together: take egges and breake them and doe away the one halfe of the whites, and after they are beaten put to them a good quantity of sweet Creame, Currants, Cinamon, Cloves, mace, Salt, and a little Ginger, Spinage, endive, and marygold flowers grossely chopt, and beate them all very well together: Then take pigges pettitoes slic't and grossely chopt, and mix them with the egges, and with your hand stirre them exceeding well together: then put sweet butter in your frying pan, and being melted, put in all the rest, and frie it browne without burning, ever and anon turning it till it be fried enough: then dish it up upon a flat plate, and cover it with suger, and so serve it foorth, Onely herein is to be observed that your pettitoes must be very well boiled before you put them into the fry-case.

And in this manner as you make this Quelquechose, so you may make any other, whether it be of flesh, smal birds, sweet rootes, oisters, muskles, cockles, giblets, lemmons, orenges, or any fruit, pulse, or other sallat herbe whatsoever: of which to speake severally were a labour infinite, because they vary with mens opinions: Onely the composition and worke is no other then this before prescribed, and who can doe these, neede no instruction for the rest.

✣ ✣ ✣

8 eggs
4–5 pigs' feet, cooked and diced
2 tablespoons heavy cream
1 teaspoon salt
¼ teaspoon freshly ground pepper
¼ teaspoon each cinnamon and cloves
⅛ teaspoon mace
pinch of ginger
2 tablespoons currants
1 pound fresh spinach, cleaned, cooked and drained
2–3 nasturtium, marigold or squash blossoms
4 tablespoons butter for frying
orange and lemon wedges for garnish

In a large bowl beat the eggs. Blend in the remaining ingredients with the exception of the butter and fruit wedges. Melt the butter in a large frying pan or skillet. Pour in half the mixture and cook until bubbly and browned on the underside. Turn and brown the other side or simply fold over like an omelet. Transfer to a serving platter and keep warm. Cook the second half of the mixture in the same manner. If pigs' feet are not available a variety of different substitutes can be made, such as ham, baby clams, chicken or shrimp. Serve garnished with orange and lemon wedges.

Serves 6

To fry an Egge as round as a Ball

Take a broad posnet or a deepe frying-panne and a quart or three pints of clarified butter or sweete suet, heate it as hot as you doe to fry Fritters, then take a sticke and stirre it till it run round like unto a whirley-pit, then breake an egge into the middle of the whirle and turne it round with your sticke untill it bee as hard as soft pocht egge, and the whirling of your suet will make it as round as a ball, then take it up with a slice and put it into a warme pipken and set it leaning against the fire, for so you may doe as many as you please, and they will keepe hot halfe an houre at the least and yet be soft.

✣ ✣ ✣

1 or 2 eggs per person
1 lb. lard

Heat the lard in a very deep frying pan until it spits when a small piece of bread is dropped into it. With a large wooden spoon stir the lard until a great pit is swirling in the center of the pan. Continue stirring and drop an egg into the center, stirring around the egg until it is cooked through. Remove gently with the slotted spoon and place the egg into a warmed casserole. Proceed with each egg until they are all cooked. It may take two people to cook eggs this way, one to crack and drop the egg, the other to stir. Serve at once.

Pyes

To make a Pye of Humbles

Take your humbles being perboiled, and choppe them verye small with a good quantitye of Mutton sewet, and halfe a handfull of hearbes folowing; time, margarom, borage, perseley, and a little rosemary, and season the same being chopped, with pepper, cloves, and mace, and so close your pye and bake him.

✣ ✣ ✣

- 1 pound tripe
- 2 tablespoons butter, melted
- 1 tablespoon parsley, chopped
- ½ teaspoon each thyme, rosemary, marjoram and borage
- ¼ teaspoon each cloves, mace and freshly ground pepper
- pinch of salt
- ¼ cup dry white wine
- pastry for a 9-inch two-crust pie (page 69)

Parboil the tripe for 15 minutes. Drain the tripe, reserving ¼ cup of the liquid. Slice the tripe into strips and mix in the butter, parsley, herbs, spices, salt, pepper, wine and the reserved liquid. Spread the mixture in the unbaked pastry shell and cover with the second crust. Seal the edges and prick the top with a fork to allow steam to escape. Bake in a preheated 350° oven for 30–40 minutes or until the crust is golden brown.

Serves 4–6

To bake a Chickin Pie

To bake a Chickin Pie after you have trust your Chickins, broken their legges and breast bones; and raised your crust of the best past, you shall lay them in the coffin close together with their bodies full of butter: Then lay upon them and underneath them currants, great raysons, prunes, cinamon, sugar, whole mace and salt: Then cover all with great store of butter and so bake it, after powre into it the same liquor you did in your marrow bone Pie, with the yelkes of 2 or 3 egges beaten amongst it: And so serve it foorth.

✣ ✣ ✣

1 pound skinned and boned chicken
2 tablespoons butter, melted
¼ cup raisins
¼ cup currants
8 prunes, chopped
1 tablespoon sugar
½ teaspoon mace
2 teaspoons salt
1 teaspoon cinnamon
½ cup sweet white wine
½ teaspoon rosewater
¼ cup broth
2 eggs, slightly beaten
pastry for a 9-inch, two-crust pie (page 69)

Place the chicken in a saucepan and cover with water. Simmer for 15 minutes, or until just barely tender. In the meantime, combine the butter, raisins, currants, prunes, sugar, mace, salt, cinnamon, wine and rosewater in a large bowl and allow the fruit to marinate until the chicken is done. Drain the chicken, reserving ¼ cup of the broth. Dice the meat and add it with the reserved broth to the fruit mixture. Add the eggs and mix well. Spread the mixture in the unbaked pastry shell, cover with the second crust and seal the edges. Prick the crust to allow steam to escape. Bake in a preheated 375° oven for about 40 minutes or until the crust is brown. Delicious either hot or cold.

Serves 4–6

To make a Tart of Spinnage

Take some cast creame, and seeth some Spinnage in faire water till it be verie soft, then put it into a Collender, that the water may soake from it: then straine the Spinnage, and cast the creame together, let there be good plentie of Spinnage: set it upon a chafingdish of coales, and put to it Sugar and some Butter, and let it boyle a while. Then put it in the paste, and bake it, and caste blanche powder on it, and so serve it in.

✣ ✣ ✣

- 2 10-ounce packages frozen chopped spinach or the equivalent in cooked fresh spinach, chopped
- ¾ cup sour cream
- 2 tablespoons butter, melted
- 2 teaspoons sugar
- 1 teaspoon salt
- ¼ teaspoon freshly ground pepper
- pastry for a 9-inch two-crust pie (page 69)

Cook the spinach according to package instructions and drain thoroughly. Blend in the remaining ingredients and spread the mixture in the unbaked pastry shell. Cover with the second crust, seal the edges and prick the top with a fork to allow steam to escape. Bake in a preheated 375° oven for 40 minutes or until the crust is golden brown. Delicious either hot or cold.

Serves 4–6

Vegitables

How to butter a Colle-flowre

Take a ripe Colle-floure and cut off the buddes, boyle them in milke with a little Mace while they be very tender, then poure them into a Cullender, and let the Milke runne cleane from them, then take a ladle full of Creame, being boyled with a little whole Mace, putting to it a Ladlefull of thicke butter, mingle them together with a little Sugar, dish up your flowres upon sippets, poure your butter and creame hot upon it strowing on a little slicst Nutmeg and salt, and serve it to the Table hot.

✣ ✣ ✣

1 head cauliflower
2 cups milk
2 tablespoons mace
3 tablespoons butter, melted
1 cup heavy cream
1 egg yolk
1 tablespoon sugar
½ teaspoon nutmeg
½ teaspoon salt

Remove the outer leaves and stalk from the cauliflower and divide it into buds. Place the buds in a saucepan, cover with milk and add the mace. Simmer until tender (about 20 minutes). Drain the milk and reserve it for another use. In a large saucepan blend the butter and cream and add the egg yolk, sugar, nutmeg and salt. Heat the sauce over a low flame, stirring constantly, until it thickens. Add the cauliflower and toss until all the buds are well coated. Cabbage may be prepared in the same manner.

Serves 4

To make a Pudding in a Turnep

Take of the fairest and clearest Turneps, and scrape off all the outside but pare it not, and cut the stalke close off as possibly you can, then cut off a round peece of the bottome like unto the bottom of a Manchet, and then with a silver spoone take out all the in-side, but keepe the outside whole like unto a dish, then take and temper it and season it in a fine pudding very stiffe, then lay on the round bottome, and turne the bottome downeward in a faire cloath, and tye it close at the toppe, then throwe it into the beefe kettle, and in an houre it will bee boyled, then dish it up and poure on the thicke butter, and grose pepper with salt round about it and so you may serve it to the table hot.

✣ ✣ ✣

4 medium turnips
2 tablespoons butter
1 teaspoon pepper
whites of 2 eggs, slightly beaten but not stiff
1 teaspoon salt
¼ teaspoon nutmeg

Wash the turnips, cut off the stalks and a small section of the bottom so that they stand upright. Gently scrape out the inside of each turnip with a paring knife or a spoon, leaving about ⅛ inch on the sides and bottom. Set these shells aside. Place the parings from inside the turnips into a pot, cover them with water and simmer for about 15 minutes. Drain the parings and mix them with the remaining ingredients. Fill the shells with the mixture and place them upright in an ovenproof dish with ¼ to ½ inch of water. Bake them in a preheated 350° oven for 30 minutes.

Serves 4

To make a Tarte of Spennedge

Boyle your Egges and your Creame together, and then put them into a bowle, and then boyle your Spinnedge, and when they are boyled, take them out of the water and straine them into your stuffe before you straine your Creame, boyle your stuffe and them strain them all againe, and season them with suger and salt.

✣ ✣ ✣

1 pound fresh or 1 10-ounce package frozen spinach
2 eggs, slightly beaten
1 tablespoon sugar
1 teaspoon salt
¾ cups sour cream

Cook the spinach until just tender or according to package instructions. Drain well until almost no moisture remains. Stir in eggs, sugar and salt and cook for 2–3 minutes. Add the sour cream and heat the mixture just long enough to warm it through. Do not allow the spinach to come to a boil or the sour cream will curdle. Serve as a vegetable.

Serves 4

To make a made Dish of Turneps

Pare your Turnepes as you would pare a Pippin, then cut them in square pieces, an inch and a halfe long and as thicke as a Butchers pricke or skewet, put them into a pipkin with a pound of butter, and three or foure spoonefuls of strong broath, and a quarter of a pint of Vineger seasoned with a little Pepper, Ginger, Salt and Sugar, and let them stue very easily upon a soft fire, for the space of two houres or more, now and then turning them with a spoone, as occasion shall serve, but by all meanes take heede you breake them not then dish them up upon Sippets, and serve them to the Table hot.

✣ ✣ ✣

10 medium turnips, peeled and sliced lengthwise
½ cup chicken broth, double strength
½ cup (1 stick) butter
¼ cup cider vinegar
½ teaspoon freshly ground pepper
1 teaspoon ginger
¼ cup sugar
1 teaspoon salt

Place the turnip slices in a medium saucepan with the remaining ingredients. Simmer the mixture on very low heat for 30–40 minutes. Stir occasionally with a spatula being careful not to break the turnips. Serve over fried bread (p. 66).

Serves 6

A sop of Onions

Take and slice your Onions, & put them in a frying panne with a dish or two of sweete butter, and frie them together, then take a litle faire water and put into it salt and peper, and so frie them together a little more, then boile them in a little Earthen pot, putting to it a little water and sweet butter, &c. You may use Spinnage in like manner.

✣ ✣ ✣

½ cup (1 stick) butter
4 large onions, sliced into rings
salt and freshly ground pepper
1 cup sour cream
¼ teaspoon nutmeg

Melt the butter in a deep skillet and add the onions. Sauté over low heat, stirring frequently, until the onions are soft and almost transparent. Add salt and pepper to taste, sour cream and nutmeg. Heat thoroughly but do not allow the mixture to come to a boil or the sour cream will curdle. Serve as a vegetable or add broth and serve as a soup.

Serves 4

To make a made Dish of Artechokes

Take your Artechokes and pare away all the top even to the meate and boyle them in sweete broth till they be somewhat tender, and then take them out, and put them into a dishe, and seethe them with Pepper, synamon and ginger, and then put in your dishe that you meane to bake them in, and put in Marrowe to them good store, and so let them bake, and when they be baked, put in a little Vineger and butter, and sticke three or foure leaves of the Artechokes in the dishe when you serve them up, and scrape Suger on the dish.

✣ ✣ ✣

10 fresh, cooked (or one package frozen) artichoke hearts
salt
freshly ground pepper
½ teaspoon cinnamon
¼ teaspoon ginger
2 tablespoons butter
½ teaspoon wine vinegar

Place the artichoke hearts (thawed if you are using a package) in a saucepan. Sprinkle with salt and pepper to taste. Add the cinnamon, ginger, butter and vinegar and simmer until the hearts are heated through.

Serves 4

To boile Onions

Take a good many onions and cut them in foure quarters, set them on the fire in as much water as you think will boyle them tender, and when they be clean skimmed, put in a good many of small raisons, halfe a spooneful of grose pepper, a good peece of Suger, and a little Salte, and when the Onions be through boiled, beat the yolke of an Egge with Vergious, and put into your pot and so serve it upon soppes. If you will poch Egges and lay upon them.

✣ ✣ ✣

- 5 medium onions, quartered
- ½ cup raisins
- ½ teaspoon salt
- freshly ground pepper
- ½ teaspoon sugar
- 2 egg yolks
- 1 tablespoon unsweetened apple juice
- 1 poached egg and 1 slice fried bread per person

Place the onions in a saucepan, cover with water and simmer until tender (about 20 minutes). Drain the onions, reserving ½ cup of the liquid. Add the raisins, salt and pepper to taste to the onions. Blend the egg yolks with the onion liquid, sugar and the apple juice and return this mixture to the onions. Simmer for about 2 minutes until the sauce thickens slightly. Top each piece of fried bread with a poached egg and cover with the onions. To serve as a vegetable, simply omit the poached egg and bread.

Serves 4

Sauces

Sauce for a roast Capon or Turkie

To make an excellent sauce for a roast Capon; you shall take Onions and having sliced and pilled them, boile them in faire water with pepper, salt, and a fewe bred crummes: then put unto it a spoonfull or two of Claret wine, the juice of an Orenge, and three or fowre slices of a Lemmon pill; all these shred together, and so powre it upon the Capon being broake up.

✤ ✤ ✤

2 tablespoons butter
1 medium onion, chopped
½ teaspoon salt
¼ teaspoon freshly ground pepper
1 tablespoon dried bread crumbs
1 tablespoon dry sherry
juice of one orange and one lemon

Melt the butter in a saucepan and sauté the onion until it is tender. Add the remaining ingredients and simmer for about 5 minutes. Serve with 2–2½ pound roast chicken or a small roast turkey.

Sauce for Chickins

The sauce for chickins is diverse according to mens tasts, for some will onely have butter, verjuice and a little parsely rolled in their bellies mixt together; others will have butter, verjuice and sugar boild together with toasts of bread, and others will have thicke sippets with the juice of sorrell and suger mixt together.

✣ ✣ ✣

4 tablespoons butter
2 tablespoons parsley, chopped
1 teaspoon cider vinegar
  or
3 teaspoons lime juice
1 teaspoon sugar

Melt the butter in a saucepan and add the remaining ingredients. Simmer for 2–3 minutes. Serve with a 1½–2 pound roast chicken. Because this sauce is tart it is also excellent with fish.

Sauce for Veale

To make a sauce for a joint of Veale, take all kinde of sweet pot-hearbes, and chopping them very small with the yelkes of two or three egges boyle them in Vinegar and Butter, with a fewe bread crummes and good store of Currants; then season it with Sugar and Cinamon, and a Clove or two crusht, and so powre it upon the veale with the slices of Orenges and Lemmons about the dish.

✣ ✣ ✣

2 tablespoons butter
2 egg yolks
1 teaspoon each sweet basil, thyme and chopped chives
1 pinch rosemary
1/4 cup wine vinegar
2 teaspoons dried bread crumbs
2 tablespoons currants
1 tablespoon sugar
1/4 teaspoon each cinnamon and cloves

Melt the butter in the top half of a double boiler. Add the egg yolks, stir well, then blend in the remaining ingredients. Heat the sauce for about two minutes, stirring constantly and being careful not to allow the egg yolks to cook too rapidly. This recipe makes a very thick sauce. For a thinner sauce use only one egg yolk and omit the bread crumbs. Serve with veal roast.

Sallets

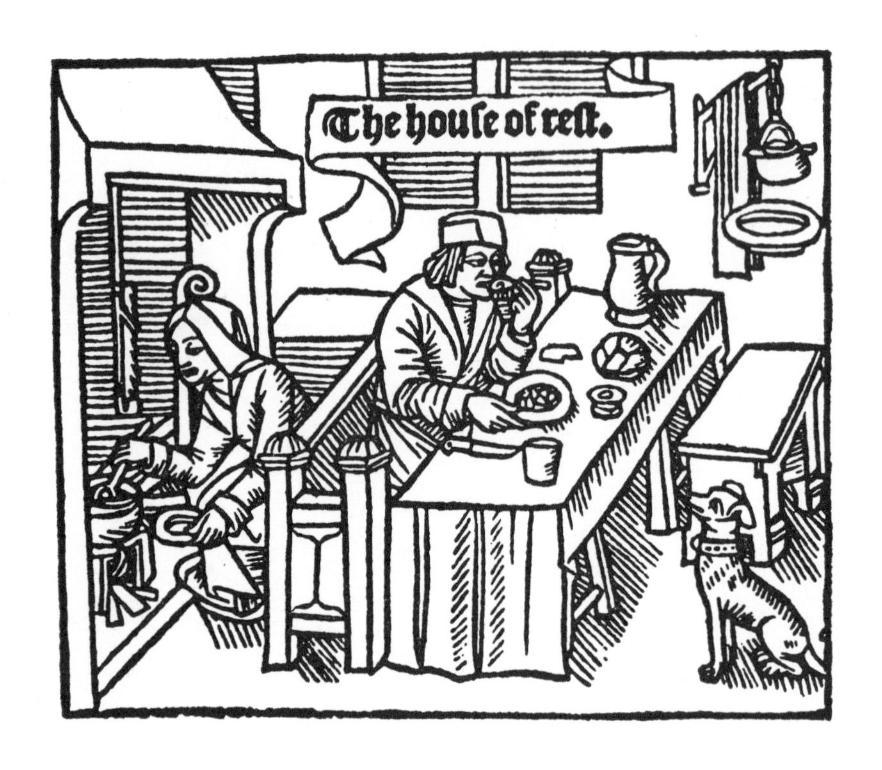
The house of rest.

Salads, by their very nature, offer an opportunity to exercise the imagination; cooked or raw foods, meats, vegetables, fruits, herbs, and even flowers all qualify as raw materials. The Elizabethans exploited this prerogative to its fullest, applying it to an unparalleled variety of ingredients and combinations—all demonstrated in the following section.

From the most unpretentious "simple Sallet," calling for only one or two ingredients, to the most elaborate centerpiece "usuall at greate feasts," each recipe holds a verbal surprise and the promise of a culinary treat. The recipes are reproduced in their fanciful, original form. Adaptation would scarcely improve their usefulness, as proportions and quantities are largely a matter of taste in salad preparation. The language is thoroughly readable; the glossary will assist in deciphering any words less than obvious.

Simple Sallets and compound Sallets

First then to speake of Sallets, there be some simple and some compounded; some onely to furnish out the table, and some both for use and adornation:

Your simple sallets are Chibols pilled, washt cleane, and halfe of the green tops cut cleane away, so serv'd on a Fruit dish, or Chines, Scallions, Radish-roots, boyled Carrets, skirrets, and Turneps, with such like served up simply; also, all young Lettice, Cabage lettice, Purslan, and divers other hearbes which may bee served simply without anything, but a little Vinegar, Sallet oyle, and Suger:

Onions boiled and stript from their rinde, and served up with Vinegar, Oyle, and Pepper is a good simple Sallet; so is Samphire, Beane-cods, Sparagus, and Coucumbers, served in likewise with Oyle, Vinegar and Pepper, with a world of others, too tedious to nominate.

Your compound Sallets, are first the young Buds and knots of all manner of wholsome hearbes at their first springing; as Redde-sage, Mints, Lettice, Violets, Marigolds, Spynage, and many others mixed together and then served up to the table with Vinegar, Sallet oyle and Sugar.

Sallet for Fish Daies

First a sallet of green fine hearbs, putting Perriwincles among them with oyle and vineger.

Another

Olives and Capers in one dish, with vineger and oyle.

Another

White Endive in a dish with perriwincles upon it, and oyle and vineger.

Another

Carret rootes being minced, and then made in the dish, after the proportion of a Flowerdeluce, then picke shrimps and lay upon it with oyle and viniger.

Another

Onions in flakes laid round about the dishe, with minced carrets laid in the middle of the dish, with boyled Hippes in five partes like an Oken leafe, made and garnished with tawney long cut with oile and vineger.

Another

Alexander buds cut long waies, garnished with welkes.

Another

Skirret rootes cut long waies in a dish with tawney long cutte, vineger and Oyle.

Another

Salmon cut long waies, with slices of onions laid upon it, and upon that to cast violets, oyle and vineger.

Another

Take pickelde Herrings and cut them long waies, and so lay them in a dish, and serve them with oyle and vineger.

Simple Sallets

. . . young Lettice, Cabage lettice, Purslan, and divers other hearbes which may bee served simply without anything, but a little Vinegar, Sallet oyle, and Suger: Onions boiled and stript from their rinde, and served up with Vinegar, Oyle, and Pepper is a good simple Sallet.

To make a Sallet of Lemmons

Cut out slices of the peele of the Lemmons long waies, a quarter of an inche one peece from an other, and then slice the Lemmon very thinne, and lay him in a dish crosse, and the peeles about the Lemmons, and scrape a good deale of suger upon them, and so serve them.

To make a Sallet of all kinde of Hearbes

Take your hearbes and picke them very fine into faire water, and picke your flowers by themselves, and washe them all cleane, and swing them in a strainer, and when you put them into a dish, mingle them with Cowcumbers or Lemmons paired and sliced, and scrape Suger, and put in vineger and Oyle, and throwe the flowers on the toppe of the sallet, and of every sorte of the aforesaide things, and garnish the dish about with foresaide thinges, and harde Egges boyled and laide about the dish and upon the sallet.

To compound an excellent Sallet, and which indeede is usuall at great Feasts, and upon Princes Tables

Take a good quantity of blaunch't Almonds, and with your Shredding knife cut them grosly; then take as manie Raisyns of the sunne cleane washt, and the stones pick't out, as many Figges shred like the Almonds, as many Capers, twise so many Olives, and as many Currants as of all the rest cleane washt: a good handfull of the small tender leaves of red Sage and Spinage; mixe all these well together with a good store of Sugar and lay them in the bottome of a great dish, then put unto them Vinegar and Oyle, and scrape more Sugar over all; then take Orenges and Lemmons, and paring away the outward pills, cut them into thinne slices, then with those slices cover the sallet all over; which done, take the thin leafe of the red Coleflowre, and with them cover the Orenges and Lemmons all over, then over those red leaves lay another course of old Olives, and the slices of wel pickld Coucumbers, together with the very inward hart of your Cabbage lettice cut into slices, then adorne the sides of the dish and the top of the Sallet with more slices of Lemons and Orenges and so serve it up.

Sallets for shew only

Now for Sallats for shewe only and the adorning and setting out of a table with numbers of dishes; they bee those which are made of Carret roots of sundrie colours well boiled and cut into many shapes and proportions, as some into knots, some in the manner of Scutchions and Armes, some like Birds, and some like wilde beasts, according to the art and cunning of the workman and these for the most part are seasoned with Vinegar, Oyle, and a little pepper.

Of preserving of Sallets

Your preserved Sallets are of two kinds, either pickeld as are Coucumbers, Samphire, Purslan, Broome, and such like, or preserved with vinegar as Violets, Primrose, Cowslops, Gillyflowers of all kinds, Broome-flowers, and for the most part, any wholsome flower whatsoever.

Now for the pickling of Sallets, they are onely boyled, and then drained from the water, spread upon a table, and good store of salt thrown over them, then when they are thorough colde make a pickle with water, salt and a little vinegar, and with the same pot them up in close earthen pots, and serve them forth as occasion shall serve.

Sweetes & Breads

The making of a fine Manchet

Take halfe a bushell of fine flower twise boulted, and a gallon of faire luke warm water, almost a handful of white salt, and almost a pinte of yest, then temper all these together, without any more liquour, as hard as you can handle it: then let it lie halfe an hower, then take it up, and make your Manchetts, and let them stande almost an hower in the oven. Memorandum, that of every bushell of meale may be made five and twentie caste of bread and everie loafe to way a pounde beside the chesill.

✣ ✣ ✣

- 2 quarter ounce packages yeast
- 1 teaspoon sugar
- 1¼ cups water
- ½ teaspoon salt
- 2 tablespoons honey
- 2 cups each unbleached white and whole wheat flour

Proof the yeast in ¼ cup of water (about 80°) with the sugar for about 10 minutes. Place in a large bowl and blend in the remaining water, the salt and the honey. Sift in 2 cups of flour, stirring constantly. Beat the mixture for about 5 minutes until it is very smooth. Continue to beat in flour until the dough is stiff enough to turn out onto a floured board. Knead the dough, gradually adding the remaining flour, for about 15 minutes or until the dough is smooth and elastic. Pat into a ball and place in a well-greased bowl. Cover with a tea towel, set in a warm place and let rise for about 1 hour or until double in bulk. Punch the dough down, knead several times and shape into a loaf. Place in a greased loaf pan, cover with towel and let rise a second time for about an hour or until double in bulk. Bake for 50–60 minutes in a preheated 400° oven. The loaf is done if it sounds hollow when tapped with a knife. Remove from pan and cool.

Yield: one loaf

To make Shrewsbery Cakes

Take a quart of very fine flower, eight ounces of fine sugar beaten and cersed, twelve ounces of sweete butter, a Nutmegge grated, two or three spoonefuls of damaske rosewater, worke all these together with your hands as hard as you can for the space of halfe an houre, then roule it in little round Cakes, about the thicknesse of three shillings one upon another, then take a silver Cup or a glasse some foure or three inches over, and cut the cakes in them, then strow some flower upon white papers & lay them upon them, and bake them in an Oven as hotte as for Manchet, set up your lid till you may tell a hundredth, then you shall see the white, if any of them rise up clap them downe with some cleane thing, and if your Oven be not too hot set up your lid againe, and in a quarter of an houre they will be baked enough, but in any case take heede your Oven be not too hot, for they must not looke browne but white, and so draw them foorth & lay them one upon another till they bee could, and you may keep them halfe a yeare the new baked are best.

✥ ✥ ✥

½ cup (1 stick) and 2 tablespoons butter, softened
½ cup sugar
¼ teaspoon rosewater
2 tablespoons water
1 cup each whole wheat and unbleached white flour
½ teaspoon nutmeg
½ teaspoon salt

Cream the butter and sugar. Add the water and rosewater and blend thoroughly. Sift together the flour, nutmeg and salt and stir into the butter just until all the ingredients are moistened and the dough holds together. Be careful to handle the dough as little as possible. Turn it out onto a floured board and roll it out to a thickness of ¼ inch. Cut large round cookies. Place the cookies on a greased cookie sheet and bake in a preheated 350° oven for 10 minutes. Turn the heat down to 300° and bake an additional 10 minutes. Remove the cookies to a rack and allow them to cool. The cookies are best when fresh, but will keep well in a tightly covered jar.

Yield: 18 cookies

Soppes

First take Butter, and melt it upon a chafingdish with coales, and lay in the dish thinne tostes of breade, and make Sorrell sauce with vergious and Gooseberries, seeth them with a litle Vergious and lay them uppon.

✣ ✣ ✣

- 4 thick slices manchet or other homemade white bread with a crisp crust
- 4 tablespoons butter
- 1 tablespoon lemon juice or unsweetened apple juice
- 1 tablespoon sugar

Melt the butter in a frying pan. Fry the bread slices for about 2 minutes or until well browned. Add the juice, turn the slices and fry an additional minute. Sprinkle with the sugar and serve with any recipe that calls for fried bread.

To make fine Cakes

Take fine flowre and good Damaske water you must have no other liquor but that, then take sweet butter, two or three yolkes of egges and a good quantity of Suger, and a fewe cloves, and mace, as your Cookes mouth shall serve him, and a lyttle saffron, and a little Gods good about a sponfull if you put in too much they shall arise, cutte them in squares lyke unto trenchers, and pricke them well, and let your oven be well swept and lay them uppon papers and so set them into the oven. Do not burne them if they be three or foure dayes olde they bee the better.

✣ ✣ ✣

3 tablespoons butter, softened
¼ cup sugar
3 egg yolks
¼ teaspoon rosewater
5 teaspoons water
1¼ cup unbleached white flour
¼ teaspoon salt
¼ teaspoon each cloves and mace
⅛ teaspoon saffron
½ teaspoon baking powder

Cream the butter and sugar. Add the egg yolks and beat again. Blend in the water and rosewater. Sift together the flour, salt, cloves, mace, saffron and baking powder. Slowly stir the flour into the butter just until all the ingredients are moistened and the dough holds together. Turn the dough onto a floured board and roll it out to a thickness of ¼ inch. Cut squares with a floured knife. Place the squares on a greased cookie sheet and prick them with a fork for decoration. Bake them in a preheated 300° oven for 15 minutes. The cakes are best when fresh, but will keep well in a tightly covered jar for about a week.

Yield: 2 dozen tea cakes

To make Jambles

Take eight ounces of flower dryed in an Oven, foure ounces of hard Sugar beaten and cerst, one ounce of Aniseede being dryed and rubd betweene your hands, the dust taken cleane out, mixe all these together with the whites of two new laid egges, and as much damaske-rose-water as will worke it with a good temperate past, then roule it in long roules as big as your little finger, then cast it into Letters or Knots of what fashion you please, so pricke with a Needle and bake it in an Oven upon white papers as hot as for Manchet, and in a quarter of an houre they will bee enough, and then Box them and keepe them dry all the yeare long for your use, and let them not bee browne in any case.

✣ ✣ ✣

1 cup unbleached white flour
½ cup sugar
pinch of salt
1 teaspoon anise seed
2 egg whites
¼ teaspoon rosewater
1 tablespoon water

Sift the flour, sugar and salt into a bowl. Add the anise seed to the flour, rubbing it between your hands to release the flavor. Beat the egg whites stiff and fold them carefully into the flour mixture. Add the rosewater and just enough water to make a workable dough. With floured hands work the dough into long rolls. Shape the rolls into letters and figures. Place these on a greased cookie sheet and prick them with a fork for decoration. Bake the cookies in a preheated 350° oven for 10–15 minutes or until they are done but not browned. Remove to a rack immediately. The cookies are best when fresh, but will keep well in a tightly covered jar for a couple of weeks.

Yield: about 10 large cookies

To make fine Paste

Take faire flower and wheate, & the yolkes of egges with sweet Butter, melted, mixing all these together with your hands, till it be brought dowe paste, & then make your coffins whether it be for pyes or tartes, then you may put Saffron and suger if you will have it a sweet paste, having respect to the true seasoning some use to put to their paste Beefe or Mutton broth, and some Creame.

✣ ✣ ✣

¾ cup unbleached white flour
4 tablespoons butter
1 egg yolk
2 tablespoons ice water

Sift the flour into a bowl. Cut in the butter with a pastry cutter or two knives until the mixture is crumbly. Add the egg yolk, blend gently. Add the water in drops. Pat the pastry into a ball and roll out on a floured board or press the pastry into a pie dish with your fingers. Chill thoroughly. For sweet pies, 2 tablespoons of sugar can be added to the recipe and for savory pies, 1 tablespoon sour cream. If the recipe calls for a baked pie shell, line the pastry with a round of waxed paper, fill with raw rice and bake in a preheated 375° oven for 15–20 minutes.

Yield: 1 9-inch pastry shell

To make an Apple Moye

Take Apples, and cut them in two or foure peeces, boyle them till they be soft, and bruise them in a morter, and put thereto the yolks of two Eggs, and a litle sweet butter, set them on a chafingdish of coales, and boyle them a litle, and put thereto a litle Sugar, synamon and Ginger, and so serve them in.

✣ ✣ ✣

- 8–10 apples
- ¼ cup water
- 2 egg yolks
- 2 tablespoons butter
- 1 teaspoon each cinnamon and ginger
- ½ cup sugar

Peel and core the apples, quarter them and place them in a saucepan with the water. Bring to a boil, then simmer for about 20 minutes or until tender. Mash the apples with a fork and blend in the egg yolks, butter, spices and sugar. Cook over a very low heat, stirring occasionally, for another 10 minutes. Serve hot or chilled.

Serves 4–6

To make Snowe

Take a quart of thicke creame, and five or sixe whites of Egs, a sawcerfull of sugar, and a sawcerfull of Rosewater, beate all together, and ever as it riseth take it out with a spoone: then take a loafe of bread, cut away the crust, and set it upright in a platter. Then set a faire great Rosemarie bush in the middest of your bread: then lay your snow with a spoon upon your Rosemary, & upon your bread, & gilt it.

✣ ✣ ✣

6 egg whites
½ pint heavy cream
½ cup sugar
¼ teaspoon rosewater
1 10 x 14-inch gingerbread
1 branch of mint or rosemary

Whip the egg whites until stiff. Slowly add the cream and continue whipping. Whip in the sugar and rosewater until the mixture is light and fluffy (about 5 minutes). Place the gingerbread on a serving platter and stick the herb branch in the center. With a spatula, spread the snow evenly over the gingerbread and dot the branch. Sprinkle dill or mint leaves around the base to resemble grass.

Serves 6–8

To make a Tarte of Strawberries

Wash your strawberies, and put them into your Tarte, and season them with suger, cynamon and Ginger, and put in a little red wine into them.

✣ ✣ ✣

1 quart strawberries
½ cup full-bodied red wine
½ cup sugar
1 teaspoon each ginger and cinnamon
1 tablespoon cornstarch
1 baked 9-inch pie shell (page 69)
whipped cream

Wash the strawberries, remove the stems and allow them to drain well. In a saucepan, heat the wine, sugar, ginger and cinnamon. Dissolve the cornstarch in just enough of the wine mixture to make a smooth paste. Add this to the saucepan and bring the wine to a boil, stirring constantly. Simmer for about 3 minutes or until the sauce thickens. Arrange the strawberries in the pie shell and pour over the syrup. Chill thoroughly. Serve the tart with whipped cream.

Serves: 6

To make a Tart of Ryce

Boyle your Rice, and put in the yolkes of two or three Egges into the Rice, and when it is boyled, put it into a dish, and season it with Suger, Sinamon and Ginger, and butter, and the juice of two or three Orenges, and set it on the fire againe.

✣ ✣ ✣

2 cups rice
3 egg yolks, slightly beaten
1 teaspoon each ginger and cinnamon
1 teaspoon salt
3 tablespoons butter
juice of 3 oranges
½ cup brown sugar

Cook the rice until it is tender. Add the remaining ingredients and mix well. Continue to cook over low heat for about five minutes, stirring constantly. Chill thoroughly before serving.

Serves 6

To make the best Panperdy

Take a dozen egges, and breake them and beat them very well, then put unto them cloves, mace, cinamon, nutmeg, and good store of suger, with as much salt as shall season it: then take a manchet and cut it into thicke slices like tostes; which done take your frying pan and put into it good store of sweet butter, and being melted lay in your slices of bread, then powre upon them one halfe of your egges, then when that is fried with a dish turne your slices of bread upward, and then powre on them the other halfe of your egges, and so turne them till both sides be browne: then dish it up and serve it with suger strowed upon it.

✣ ✣ ✣

6 eggs
½ teaspoon salt
pinch of cloves, mace, nutmeg and cinnamon
4 tablespoons butter
½ loaf french bread, cut into ¾-inch slices
brown sugar

Beat the eggs until foamy; add the salt and spices. Melt the butter in a wide frying pan and drop in the bread slices. Pour half the egg mixture over the bread; fry for 2–3 minutes or until the eggs harden. Lift the bread from the pan, melt the remaining butter and turn the bread slices back into the pan. Pour over the remaining egg mixture and cook for an additional 2–3 minutes. Serve with butter and brown sugar.

Serves 4

The best Pancake

To make the best Pancake, take two or three egges, and breake them into a dish, and beate them well: Then adde unto them a pretty quantity of faire running water, and beate all well together: Then put in cloves, mace, cinamon, and a nutmegge, and season it with salt; which done make it thicke as you thinke good with fine wheate flower: Then frie the cakes as thinne as may bee with sweete butter, or sweete seame, and make them browne, and so serve them up with sugar strowed upon them. There be some which mixe Pancakes with new milke or creame, but that makes them tough, cloying, and not so crispe, pleasant and savory as running water.

✣ ✣ ✣

3 eggs
¼ cup water
1 cup milk
2 tablespoons butter, melted
¼ cup sugar
pinch of salt
¼ teaspoon each cloves, nutmeg and mace
2 teaspoons cinnamon
1½ cups whole wheat flour
butter or salad oil for frying

Beat the eggs until foamy. Add the water, milk, and butter. Blend together the sugar, salt and spices and add to the liquids. Slowly add enough flour to make a thin batter. Heat the butter or salad oil in a frying pan until a drop of batter sizzles. Pour in batter and spread as thin as possible, turning as soon as the pancakes are brown. The thinner the batter, the faster the cooking and the better the taste. Serve hot with butter and sugar.

Yield: 15–18 filling pancakes

To make a Trifle

Take a pinte of thicke Creame, and season it with Sugar and Ginger, and Rosewater, so stirre it as you would then have it, and make it luke warme in a dish on a Chafingdishe and coales, and after put it into a silver peece or a bowle, and so serve it to the boorde.

✣ ✣ ✣

1 pint whipping cream
¼ cup sugar
2 drops rosewater
¼ teaspoon ginger

Whip the cream, add the sugar and whip again until well blended. Stir in rosewater and ginger. Serve as is, over sponge cake, or with sliced fresh fruit.

Serves 4–6

Drinkes

To make Ipocras

To make Ipocras take a pottell of wine, two ounces of good Cinamon, halfe an ounce of ginger, nine cloves, and sixe pepper cornes, and a nutmeg, and bruise them and put them into the wine with some rosemary flowers, and so let them steepe all night, and then put in sugar a pound at least; and when it is well setled let it runne through a woollen bag made for that purpose: thus if your wine be clarret, the Ipocras will be red, if white then of that colour also.

✥ ✥ ✥

2 quarts red wine
1 tablespoon ginger
2 tablespoons cinnamon
½ teaspoon nutmeg
6 whole peppercorns
9 whole cloves
½ teaspoon rosemary
1 cup sugar

Pour the wine into a large glass jar. Add the ginger, cinnamon and nutmeg. With a mortar and pestle crush the peppercorns, cloves and rosemary. Add these and the sugar to the wine. Cover and let stand for at least 12 hours. Strain the wine before serving. The wine can be chilled or heated before serving.

Serves 10

Buttered Beere

Take three pintes of Beere, put five yolkes of Egges to it, straine them together, and set it in a pewter pot to the fyre, and put to it halfe a pound of Sugar, one penniworth of Nutmegs beaten, one penniworth of Cloves beaten, and a halfepenniworth of Ginger beaten, and when it is all in, take another pewter pot and brewe them together, and set it to the fire againe, and when it is readie to boyle, take it from the fire, and put a dish of sweet butter into it, and brewe them together out of one pot into an other.

✣ ✣ ✣

3 pints beer
3 tablespoons sugar
⅛ teaspoon each nutmeg and cloves
pinch of ginger
2 tablespoons unsalted butter

Pour the beer into a saucepan. Add all the ingredients except the butter and simmer for about 5 minutes. Remove from the heat and drop in the butter. Allow the butter to melt and serve immediately. Good for parties or on cold, wintery evenings.

Serves 4

Sample Menus

Breakfast or Brunch

The best Pancake
To make an Apple Moye

To fry an Egge as round as a Ball
To fry Bakon to serve with these Egges
To make Shrewsbery Cakes

To make Egs upon Sops
Fresh fruit

To butter Egges of the best Fashion
To make a Tarte of Strawberries
Manchet

Luncheon

To bake a Trout
To make a Sallet of all kinde of Hearbes

To make a Quelquechose
Sallet for Fish Daies

Dinner

To roste Olives of Veale
A Sop of Onion
A Sallet (Carret rootes and Shrimps)
To make a Tarte of Strawberries
Manchet
Ale or Beere

To boile a Breame
To make a Tarte of Spennedge
A Sallet (Endive with Perriwincles)
Manchet
Fresh fruit

To stew Fillets of Beefe
How to butter a Colle-flowre
To make a Sallet of Lemmons
Manchet
Ale or Beere

To roste a Hare
To make a made Dish of Turneps
To make a Sallet of all kinde of Hearbes
Manchet
Beere

To boile a Capon with Orenges and Lemmons
A Sallet (Olives and Capers)
To make a made Dishe of Artechokes
To make a Tart of Ryce
Manchet
Ale or Beere

Parties and Holidays

To bake Venison
To frie Chickins
To seeth fresh Salmon
Simple Sallets
Manchet
Fresh fruit
Ale and Beere

To boyle Chickens with Sparagus
To make stewed Steaks
To stew Flounders
To boile Onions
To make Snowe
Ipocras
Manchet

Glossary

Alexanders–A plant with clusters of small yellow flowers, formerly cultivated and eaten as celery

Bakon–Fresh flesh, now called pork; the cured hind of the pig

Barm–Froth at top of fermenting malt liquors; used to leaven bread and to cause fermentation in other liquors; yeast or leaven

Blanche powder–Ground spices blended with sugar

Boulted–Sifted

Breame–Bream; a freshwater fish of yellowish color and with an arched back

Broaching–Putting meat on a spit for roasting

Broch–A spit for roasting

Broome–Broom; a plant bearing large yellow flowers which flourishes in sandy soil

Bruise–To crush or grate

Butcher's prick–A sharpened stick or piece of metal used to spear pieces of meat; skewer

Cerse–Sift (also: sarse)

Chesill–Small pebbles, gravel or shingle

Chibols–A species of Allium, known also as stone leek, rock onion and welsh onion; looks like a cross between an onion and a leek

Chine–Backbone or a cut of meat containing some of the backbone

Coffin–Pie crust or pie dish

Faggot–A bundle (of herbs); bouquet garni

Flowerdeluce–Fleur-de-lis

Gods Good–Barm, yeast

Hippes–Rose hips; fruit of the wild rose, or of any rose

Humbles–Innards of a deer or other large animal; tripe

Hypocrase–See Ipocras

Iambales–A kind of sweet cake or bisquit, usually made in the form of rings or rolls

Ipocras–A cordial drink of wine and spices (also: Hypocrase)

Lid–Top crust of a pie

Manchet–Finest quality of Elizabethan bread made from wheat flour

Marie bones–Marrow bones

Moye–A dish made from stewed apples

Olives–Dish composed of thin slices of beef or veal, rolled up with onions and herbs and stewed in brown sauce

Panperdy–A fancy bread dish similar to French toast (from the French *pain perdu*)

Paste–Pie pastry, dough

Penniworth–A very small amount

Pigges Pettitoes–Pigs' feet

Pipkin–Small earthenware pot

Pippin–A type of apple

Posnet–A small metal pot or vessel for boiling, having a handle and three feet

Pottle–Two quarts

Pudding–The stomach or entrails of an animal stuffed with seasonings and meats and stored for longer periods; a kind of sausage; stuffing put into the cavity of an animal before roasting

Purslan–Purslane; a succulent herb, seldom found in modern kitchens

Quelquechose–A fancy dish, with an egg base, composed of a great variety of ingredients; of French origin

Roste–Roast

Sacke–A class of dry white wines produced in Spain and the Canary Islands in the 16th century

Sallet–Salad

Samphire–Glasswort; a plant found on rocks by the sea, usually used as a pickling spice

Sarse–Sift or strain (also: cerse)

Scutchion–Scutcheon; a shield-shaped object

Seame (*seam*)–To dress with grease or fat; to grease with hog's lard

Seethe–Boil

Sippets–Pieces of toasted or fried bread (also: sops, soppes)

Skirret–A species of water parsnip, the tubers or roots of which were eaten

Snowe–A fluffy confection made from whipped egg whites

Soppes–See Sippets

Sorrell sauce–The juice of crushed and strained sorrel; a tart sauce

Straine–To sift or strain

Sweete butter–Unsalted butter

Tart (*tarte*)–A pie in the modern sense, with one or two crusts and a sweet or savory filling; also, a vegetable or sweet dish bound with cream or eggs

Tawney–Tansy; a plant with bitter taste; both plant and flowers are edible

Trencher–Piece of wood, circular or square and hollowed out for use as a plate or cutting surface for meat, one side was flat and could be used for a second course

Trifle–A dish composed of cream boiled with various ingredients

Verjuice (*vergious*)–Unsweetened juice of green or unripe grapes, crabapples or other sour fruits

Index

SALLETS, HUMBLES AND SHREWSBERY CAKES has been designed, composed, and printed by Michael and Winifred Bixler. The typeface, Monotype Dante, was designed by the archtypographer Giovanni Mardersteig. It was cut in its original version by Charles Malin and was first used by Mardersteig in 1954. The subsequent recutting by the Monotype Corporation of this strong and elegant Renaissance design preserves all the liveliness, personality, and grace of Malin's original engraving. The display type throughout is Cloister Black, a foundry face strongly reminiscent of the *lettre de forme*, the angular script in use in northern Europe and particularly Germany throughout the fifteenth and sixteenth centuries. ¶The illustrations have been reproduced from the original woodcuts found in English illustrated books of the fifteenth century. ¶This book has been printed letterpress on Ticonderoga Text and has been bound at the Stanhope Bindery, Boston. The end-papers are Linweave Text.

3000 COPIES